How to Money With Webinars: Unlocking Profitable Opportunities

Table of Contents

Introduction:

Welcome to "How to Make Money with Webinars: Unlocking Profitable Opportunities." In today's digital landscape, webinars have emerged as powerful tools for connecting with audiences, sharing valuable knowledge, and generating income. Whether you're an entrepreneur, a consultant, an educator, or someone with specialized expertise, webinars offer a platform to monetize your skills and create a sustainable income stream.

In this course, we will delve into the strategies and techniques that will help you harness the potential of webinars to maximize your financial success. From choosing the right webinar platform to promoting your sessions effectively, we will cover every aspect of the process. With a focus on creating engaging content, attracting a target audience, and implementing revenue-generating methods, this course will equip you with the knowledge and tools to thrive in the competitive world of webinar monetization.

Throughout this course, you will discover how to craft compelling webinars that captivate your audience, establish your expertise, and generate substantial revenue. We will explore various approaches, from selling your knowledge through paid webinars to leveraging affiliate marketing and sponsorship opportunities. By the end, you will have a comprehensive understanding of the strategies and tactics necessary to successfully monetize your webinars.

Whether you're just starting or already have some webinar experience, this course is designed to meet you where you are and take your webinar revenue to new heights. So, let's embark on this journey together, exploring the endless possibilities of making money with webinars. Get ready to unlock the potential of this dynamic medium and turn your expertise into a profitable venture. Let's get started!

What are webinars

Webinars are online seminars or presentations that are conducted over the internet. The term "webinar" is a combination of "web" (referring to the internet) and "seminar." They allow individuals or organizations to host live or pre-recorded interactive sessions, workshops, lectures, or presentations, and deliver them to a remote audience.

Webinars are typically used for educational, informational, or promotional purposes. They provide a convenient way for people from different locations to participate in a virtual event without the need for physical presence. Participants can join webinars using their computers, laptops, tablets, or smartphones, as long as they have an internet connection.

During a webinar, the presenter or host shares their expertise, knowledge, or information on a specific topic using slides, videos, or other multimedia content.

Participants can usually interact with the presenter through features like live chat, Q&A sessions, polls, or surveys. Some webinars also offer features such as screen sharing, whiteboards, and breakout rooms for group discussions or activities.

Webinars have become popular in various fields, including business, education, marketing, training, and professional development. They offer advantages such as cost-effectiveness, scalability, global reach, and the ability to record sessions for later viewing. Additionally, webinars can accommodate large audiences or be tailored to smaller, more intimate groups.

Overall, webinars provide a flexible and accessible way to share knowledge, engage with an audience, and foster interactive learning experiences online.

Paid webinars

Paid webinars are online seminars or presentations for which participants are required to pay a fee to attend. These webinars are usually organized by individuals, businesses, educational institutions, or organizations that offer specialized knowledge, training, or valuable information on a particular topic.

Paid webinars often provide a higher level of expertise, in-depth content, or exclusive access to industry experts compared to free webinars. They may cover topics such as professional skills development, business strategies, personal growth, industry trends, financial advice, and more. The fee charged for attending a paid webinar can vary depending on the content, duration, reputation of the presenter, and perceived value of the information provided.

When participants pay for a webinar, they typically receive additional benefits or resources beyond the live session. These benefits may include access to recorded sessions for future reference, downloadable materials, e-books, worksheets, bonus content, or exclusive membership to a community or online platform.

Paid webinars can be an effective way for experts or organizations to monetize their knowledge and provide participants with valuable insights and learning opportunities. Participants, on the other hand, benefit from the expertise and specialized information shared during the webinar, which can help them enhance their skills, knowledge, or understanding of a specific subject.

It's important to note that not all webinars are paid, and there are numerous free webinars available that offer valuable content as well. The decision to participate in a paid webinar depends on the individual's interest in the topic, the credibility of the presenter, and the perceived value of the information provided.

How to choose the right webinar platform

When choosing the right webinar platform, there are several factors to consider to ensure it meets your specific needs and objectives. Here are some key considerations:

Features and Functionality: Evaluate the features and functionality offered by different webinar platforms. Consider features such as the ability to host live or pre-recorded webinars, screen sharing, interactive tools (chat, polls, Q&A), integration with other software or platforms, audience engagement options, and analytics/reporting capabilities.

Scalability and Audience Size: Determine the scale of your webinars and the number of participants you expect. Some platforms have limitations on the number of attendees or additional costs for larger audiences. Ensure the platform can handle the anticipated number of participants without compromising performance.

Ease of Use: Look for a webinar platform that is user-friendly and intuitive, both for the host and the attendees. The interface should be easy to navigate, set up, and customize. Consider the technical expertise required to operate the platform effectively.

Reliability and Stability: Ensure the platform has a reliable infrastructure and can handle the bandwidth requirements for streaming webinars smoothly. Check for reviews or testimonials from other users to gauge the platform's stability and uptime record.

Integration and Compatibility: Consider the integration options with other tools and software you use, such as email marketing platforms, CRM systems, or learning management systems (LMS). Compatibility with different operating systems, browsers, and devices (desktop, mobile) is also essential for a broader reach.

Security and Privacy: Data security is crucial, especially when dealing with sensitive information or payment transactions during paid webinars. Look for platforms that offer encryption, secure payment gateways, and data protection measures to ensure the privacy and safety of your participants.

Cost: Evaluate the pricing plans and subscription models offered by webinar platforms. Consider factors like the number of webinars you plan to host, the size of your audience, and any additional features or services you may require. Compare pricing structures and choose a platform that aligns with your budget.

Customer Support: Consider the level of customer support provided by the platform. Look for platforms that offer responsive customer support, documentation, tutorials, and training resources to assist you in setting up and troubleshooting any issues that may arise.

Reviews and Reputation: Research and read reviews or testimonials from other users to gain insights into their experiences with the platform. Pay attention to feedback on the platform's performance, customer service, and overall user satisfaction.

By considering these factors and conducting thorough research, you can select a webinar platform that best suits your requirements, ensuring a smooth and successful webinar experience for both hosts and participants.

How to promote your webinar effectively

Promoting your webinar effectively is crucial to attract a relevant and engaged audience. Here are some strategies to help you promote your webinar successfully:

Define Your Target Audience: Identify your target audience and understand their needs, interests, and pain points. Tailor your webinar content and promotional messages to resonate with their specific interests and challenges.

Utilize Email Marketing: Build an email list of individuals who might be interested in your webinar topic. Send personalized and compelling email invitations to your contacts, highlighting the value and benefits of attending the webinar. Follow up with reminders as the webinar date approaches.

Leverage Social Media: Utilize social media platforms to reach a wider audience. Create engaging posts, videos, or graphics promoting your webinar and share them across relevant social media channels. Consider using paid social media advertising to target specific demographics or interest groups.

Collaborate with Influencers or Partners: Identify influencers or industry experts who have a relevant audience and can promote your webinar to their followers. Collaborate with them to co-host or endorse your webinar, leveraging their reach and credibility.

Create Engaging Content: Develop compelling content related to your webinar topic, such as blog posts, infographics, or videos, and share them on your website or social media channels. Use these pieces of content to generate interest, educate your audience, and drive traffic to your webinar registration page.

Utilize Webinar Listing Platforms: Submit your webinar details to relevant webinar listing directories or platforms. These platforms attract audiences looking for educational or industry-specific webinars and can help increase your visibility.

Offer Early Bird or Limited-Time Offers: Create a sense of urgency by offering early bird discounts or limited-time promotions for webinar registration. Encourage participants to sign up early to secure their spot and take advantage of exclusive offers.

Optimize Landing Pages: Create a dedicated landing page for your webinar registration with a clear and compelling call-to-action. Ensure the page is optimized for search engines, loads quickly, and provides all the necessary details about the webinar.

Engage with Your Network: Leverage your professional network, industry associations, or online communities to promote your webinar. Share information about your webinar in relevant forums, discussion groups, or online communities where your target audience is active.

Utilize Webinar Registrants: Encourage your webinar registrants to spread the word by providing social sharing buttons or referral incentives. Offer rewards or exclusive bonuses to registrants who refer others to attend the webinar.

Personalize Outreach: Reach out to individuals or organizations directly if you believe they would benefit from your webinar. Craft personalized messages highlighting the value the webinar offers to their specific needs or interests.

Follow-Up and Repurpose Content: After the webinar, follow up with attendees and provide them with post-webinar resources or recordings. Repurpose the webinar content into blog posts, videos, or social media snippets to extend the lifespan of your webinar's value and reach a wider audience.

Remember, consistency is key when promoting your webinar. Develop a comprehensive promotional plan, leverage multiple channels, and monitor the effectiveness of your strategies to make adjustments and improve future webinar promotions.

Importance of always delivering quality webinar content

Delivering quality webinar content is essential for several reasons:

Engaging and Retaining Participants: Quality content captures the attention of your audience and keeps them engaged throughout the webinar. Engaged participants are more likely to stay until the end, actively participate, and absorb the information you provide. High-quality content increases the chances of participants finding value in your webinar and becoming repeat attendees.

Building Credibility and Trust: When you consistently deliver valuable and insightful content, you establish yourself as an authority and build credibility in your field. Participants trust your expertise and knowledge, making them more likely to seek your advice or engage with your brand in the future. Quality content helps you establish a positive reputation and become a go-to resource for your audience.

Creating a Positive User Experience: Webinars with high-quality content provide a positive user experience. Participants appreciate well-structured presentations, clear explanations, and relevant examples or case studies. A positive user experience leads to higher satisfaction levels and encourages participants to share their positive experiences with others, potentially increasing the reach and impact of your webinar.

Increasing Attendee Satisfaction and Engagement: When participants find value in your webinar content, they are more likely to be satisfied with the experience. Satisfied attendees are more likely to provide positive feedback, testimonials, or reviews, helping you attract more participants in the future. Engaging and valuable content also encourages active participation, such as asking questions, providing comments, or participating in polls, fostering a dynamic and interactive webinar environment.

Generating Word-of-Mouth Referrals: Delivering quality content creates a positive impression and increases the likelihood of participants recommending your webinar to others. Word-of-mouth referrals can be a powerful marketing tool, attracting new participants who trust the recommendations of their peers. A reputation for quality content can lead to a growing audience and increased webinar attendance over time.

Supporting Brand Building and Marketing Goals: Webinars can be a part of your overall brand building and marketing strategy. Quality content aligns with your brand's values and positioning, strengthening brand awareness and recognition. Consistently delivering high-quality webinars contributes to your overall marketing efforts, demonstrating your commitment to excellence and providing a valuable touchpoint for your target audience.

Driving Business Goals: Webinars often serve specific business goals, such as generating leads, promoting products or services, or increasing customer loyalty. Quality content increases the likelihood of achieving these goals by effectively conveying the key messages, demonstrating the value of your offerings, and compelling participants to take desired actions.

In summary, delivering quality webinar content is crucial for engaging and retaining participants, building credibility and trust, creating positive user experiences, increasing attendee satisfaction and engagement, generating word-of-mouth referrals, supporting brand building and marketing goals, and driving business outcomes. By consistently providing valuable and insightful content, you can maximize the impact and success of your webinars.

Importance of eye-catching visuals in webinars

Eye-catching visuals play a significant role in webinars for several important reasons:

Capture and Maintain Attention: Attention spans are limited, especially in online environments. Eye-catching visuals help grab participants' attention and keep them engaged throughout the webinar. Colorful, visually appealing graphics, images, and slides can attract and hold participants' focus, making your content more memorable and impactful.

Enhance Comprehension and Retention: Visuals aid in information processing and understanding. They can help simplify complex concepts, illustrate ideas, and reinforce key points. Well-designed visuals, such as charts, graphs, diagrams, or infographics, can make information more accessible and easier to comprehend, increasing participants' retention of the webinar content.

Support Visual Learners: People have different learning preferences, and some individuals are more visually oriented. By incorporating eye-catching visuals, you cater to the needs of visual learners, ensuring they can absorb and understand the webinar content effectively. Visuals provide an additional avenue for conveying information beyond verbal communication alone.

Improve Recall and Recall: Engaging visuals enhance participants' ability to remember and recall information presented in the webinar. Research shows that visuals can significantly improve memory retention. When participants remember the content, they are more likely to apply the knowledge gained during the webinar to real-life situations or share it with others, increasing the webinar's impact.

Communicate Complex Concepts Efficiently: Certain concepts or processes may be challenging to explain solely through verbal communication. Eye-catching visuals allow you to simplify and communicate complex ideas more efficiently. Visual representations can break down complex concepts into digestible components, making them easier to understand and follow.

Increase Engagement and Interactivity: Eye-catching visuals can encourage active participation and interaction during the webinar. For example, you can use visuals to present poll questions, conduct quizzes, or initiate discussions. Visual elements spark interest and prompt participants to engage with the content, creating a more dynamic and interactive webinar experience.

Reflect Professionalism and Branding: Visually appealing webinar presentations demonstrate professionalism and attention to detail. Well-designed visuals reflect positively on your brand and create a cohesive visual identity. Consistent branding elements, such as colors, fonts, and graphics, contribute to brand recognition and reinforce your message.

Enhance Emotional Connection: Visuals have the power to evoke emotions and create a connection with participants. Compelling images, illustrations, or videos can elicit emotional responses, making the webinar content more relatable and memorable. This emotional connection enhances participants' engagement and their likelihood of taking desired actions.

Incorporating eye-catching visuals into your webinars is crucial for capturing attention, enhancing comprehension, supporting different learning preferences, improving recall, communicating complex concepts, increasing engagement and interactivity, reflecting professionalism and branding, and creating an emotional connection. By leveraging the power of visuals, you can make your webinars more impactful and memorable for participants.

42 Ways To Make Money From Webinars

There are several ways to monetize webinars and generate income from your webinar efforts. Here are some strategies to consider:

1. **Paid Webinars**: Offer exclusive content or specialized knowledge through paid webinars. Participants pay a fee to attend the webinar and gain access to valuable insights, training, or information. Ensure that your webinar content provides substantial value and addresses specific pain points or interests of your target audience.

Example of How to Make Money with Paid Webinars – A Case Study

Imagine you are an experienced marketer specializing in social media strategies, and you want to monetize your knowledge by offering paid webinars. Here's an example of how you can make money through paid webinars:

Identify Your Target Audience: Determine who would benefit most from your expertise in social media marketing. It could be small business owners, entrepreneurs, or marketing professionals seeking to enhance their social media presence.

Develop an Engaging Webinar Topic: Create a compelling webinar topic that addresses a specific pain point or offers valuable insights. For example, "Mastering Instagram for Business: Strategies to Boost Engagement and Drive Sales." Ensure the topic aligns with your target audience's needs and interests.

Choose a Webinar Platform: Select a reliable webinar platform that provides features such as registration management, interactive tools, and recording capabilities. Options like Zoom, GoToWebinar, or WebinarNinja offer robust features for hosting paid webinars.

Set a Competitive Price: Research the market to determine an appropriate price for your webinar. Consider the value you are providing, the duration of the webinar, and the expertise you bring to the table. Price your webinar competitively, taking into account what others in your industry charge for similar content.

Create Compelling Marketing Materials: Develop persuasive marketing materials to promote your paid webinar. Craft a captivating webinar landing page that highlights the benefits and outcomes participants can expect. Use persuasive copy, compelling visuals, and customer testimonials to build credibility and drive conversions.

Implement a Marketing Strategy: Utilize various marketing channels to reach your target audience. Leverage your email list, social media platforms, and professional networks to promote your webinar. Create engaging social media posts, run targeted ads, and reach out to relevant industry influencers for potential collaborations or endorsements.

Offer Early Bird or Limited-Time Discounts: Encourage early sign-ups by offering limited-time discounts or early bird pricing. This creates a sense of urgency and motivates participants to take action. Promote these special offers in your marketing campaigns to attract early registrations.

Deliver High-Quality Webinar Content: Ensure your webinar delivers exceptional value to participants.

Craft a well-structured presentation that educates, inspires, and equips attendees with actionable insights. Incorporate interactive elements such as polls, Q&A sessions, and downloadable resources to engage participants throughout the webinar.

Provide Additional Resources: Offer supplementary resources such as worksheets, templates, or case studies that complement your webinar content. These resources can be included as part of the paid webinar package, adding extra value for participants.

Follow Up with Upsell Opportunities: Once participants have attended your paid webinar, follow up with additional upsell opportunities. Offer them the chance to purchase related products, access to an exclusive membership community, or one-on-one coaching sessions to further their learning and implementation.

By implementing these strategies, you can generate revenue from paid webinars while providing valuable knowledge and insights to your audience. Remember to continually assess participant feedback, refine your content, and explore new topics to keep your webinar offerings fresh and engaging. With dedication and a focus on delivering value, your paid webinars can become a profitable income stream.

2. **Sponsorships and Partnerships**: Seek out sponsors or partners who are interested in reaching your webinar audience. Collaborate with relevant brands or businesses that align with your webinar topic or industry. They can provide financial support or resources in exchange for exposure during the webinar or promotional opportunities to your audience.

Illustration:

Making Money on Webinars with Sponsorships and Partnerships

Let's imagine you are a fitness expert who regularly hosts webinars on health and wellness topics. You have built a strong following and now want to explore opportunities for monetization through sponsorships and partnerships. Here's an illustration of how you can make money on webinars with sponsorships and partnerships:

Identify Potential Sponsors: Research companies that align with your niche and target audience. Look for brands that offer fitness products, health supplements, athletic apparel, or wellness services. Reach out to these companies to gauge their interest in sponsoring your webinars.

Craft a Sponsorship Proposal: Create a compelling sponsorship proposal that outlines the benefits and value your webinars can offer to potential sponsors. Highlight the size and engagement of your audience, the demographics of your followers, and the reach of your marketing channels.

Offer Different Sponsorship Packages: Develop tiered sponsorship packages that provide varying levels of exposure and benefits to sponsors. For example, you could offer different sponsorship levels like Gold, Silver, and Bronze, each with different advertising opportunities, branding visibility, and promotion during your webinars.

Display Sponsor Logos and Mention Them: During your webinars, prominently display sponsor logos on your webinar landing page, slides, and promotional materials. Acknowledge and mention your sponsors at the beginning and end of each webinar, expressing gratitude for their support and briefly discussing their products or services.

Provide Sponsored Content or Product Demonstrations: Incorporate sponsored content or product demonstrations within your webinars. Collaborate with sponsors to showcase their offerings in a way that adds value to your audience. For instance, you could demonstrate how to use a fitness device or feature a sponsored workout segment using specific fitness equipment.

Offer Sponsored Giveaways or Discounts: Collaborate with sponsors to host sponsored giveaways or offer exclusive discounts to your webinar participants. This incentivizes engagement and creates a win-win situation for both your audience and the sponsor. Participants get a chance to win valuable products or receive special discounts, while sponsors gain exposure and potential customers.

Cross-Promotion and Co-Branding Opportunities: Explore opportunities for cross-promotion and co-branding with sponsors. This could involve featuring their logo on your website or social media channels, co-creating content, or collaborating on joint marketing campaigns. Align your brand with your sponsors to create a mutually beneficial partnership that extends beyond individual webinars.

Measure and Communicate Results: Track the success of your sponsorships by measuring key metrics such as audience engagement, click-through rates, or conversions generated from your webinars. Provide regular reports and updates to your sponsors to demonstrate the value they are receiving from the partnership. This builds trust and lays the foundation for long-term collaborations.

Seek Affiliate or Referral Partnerships: Explore affiliate or referral partnerships with sponsors where you earn a commission for any sales generated through your webinar participants. This incentivizes sponsors to actively promote your webinars and can lead to increased revenue for both parties.

Evaluate and Renew Sponsorship Agreements: Regularly assess the performance of your sponsorships and partnerships. If a sponsorship is successful, consider renewing the agreement for future webinars or exploring opportunities for deeper collaboration. If a partnership isn't delivering the expected results, reassess and seek new opportunities that better align with your audience and goals.

By leveraging sponsorships and partnerships, you can monetize your webinars while providing valuable content to your audience. Remember to maintain transparency, choose sponsors that align with your values and audience, and continuously strive to deliver engaging and informative webinars. With the right collaborations, your webinars can become a profitable revenue stream while benefiting both you and your sponsors.

3. **Affiliate Marketing**: Incorporate affiliate marketing into your webinar strategy. Promote relevant products or services as an affiliate and earn commissions for each sale made through your referral. Select products or services that complement your webinar content and would genuinely benefit your audience.

Illustration: Making Money with Webinars through Affiliate Marketing

Let's imagine you are a digital marketing expert who frequently hosts webinars on various marketing strategies. You have built a loyal following, and now you want to explore opportunities to monetize your webinars through affiliate marketing. Here's an illustration of how you can make money with webinars through affiliate marketing:

Identify Relevant Affiliate Programs: Research affiliate programs that align with your webinar topics and target audience. Look for companies that offer products or services related to digital marketing, such as marketing software, online courses, website hosting, or email marketing platforms.

Join Affiliate Programs: Sign up for the affiliate programs of the companies you have identified. Typically, you will receive a unique affiliate link or promo code that tracks the sales generated through your referrals. Ensure you understand the terms and commission structure of each program.

Integrate Affiliate Offers into Webinars: Identify key points during your webinars where you can seamlessly integrate affiliate offers. For example, if you are discussing email marketing strategies, you could mention and recommend an email marketing software or training course as an affiliate offer.

Highlight Benefits and Use Cases: Clearly explain the benefits and value of the affiliate products or services to your webinar participants. Share real-life use cases, success stories, or case studies to demonstrate how they can help solve specific challenges or achieve desired outcomes.

Provide Exclusive Discounts or Bonuses: Negotiate with the affiliate companies to provide exclusive discounts or bonuses for your webinar participants. This incentivizes them to make a purchase through your affiliate link, knowing they are receiving a special offer not available elsewhere.

Display Affiliate Links and Promo Codes: Share your affiliate links or promo codes prominently during your webinar. Display them on your webinar slides, in the chatbox, or in the follow-up email. Make it easy for participants to access the offers and remember to disclose that you may earn a commission from their purchases.

Share Affiliate Resources and Materials: Request marketing collateral, product demos, or resources from the affiliate companies to share with your webinar participants. This could include whitepapers, e-books, or video tutorials that provide additional value and encourage participants to explore the affiliate products further.

Follow Up with Email Marketing: Use your email list to follow up with participants after the webinar. Send a recap email that includes the webinar recording, relevant resources, and a reminder of the affiliate offers. Personalize the email and emphasize the benefits of the affiliate products or services.

Track Affiliate Conversions and Earnings: Regularly monitor your affiliate program dashboards or reports to track conversions and earnings generated through your webinars. Evaluate which affiliate offers perform best and adjust your promotional strategies accordingly.

Continuously Optimize and Expand: Analyze the performance of your affiliate marketing efforts and refine your strategies based on participant feedback and conversion rates. Explore new affiliate partnerships, expand your offerings, and stay updated on industry trends to maximize your revenue potential.

By incorporating affiliate marketing into your webinars, you can monetize your expertise while providing valuable recommendations to your audience. Remember to be transparent about your affiliate relationships and only promote products or services that you genuinely believe in. With strategic affiliate marketing, your webinars can become a profitable income stream that benefits both you and your audience.

4. *Upselling and Cross-selling:* *Utilize webinars as a platform to showcase your products, services, or additional offerings. Provide valuable content during the webinar and use it as an opportunity to promote and sell related products* or services to participants. Emphasize the value and benefits they will receive by purchasing the upsell or cross-sell offerings.

Making Money with Webinars through Upselling and Cross-Selling

Webinars provide an excellent platform to not only share valuable content but also generate revenue through upselling and cross-selling. Here's how you can effectively make money with webinars through these techniques:

Identify Relevant Products or Services: Identify complementary products or services that align with your webinar content and offer additional value to your audience. For example, if you are hosting a webinar on social media marketing, you could consider upselling an advanced social media management tool or cross-selling a content creation course.

Plan Your Sales Funnel: Design a sales funnel that guides participants from your webinar to the upsell or cross-sell offer. The sales funnel can include steps such as offering a free resource related to the webinar topic in exchange for email addresses, nurturing leads through email campaigns, and promoting the upsell or cross-sell offer in subsequent communications.

Incorporate Soft Selling Techniques: During your webinar, subtly introduce the upsell or cross-sell offer as an additional resource that can further enhance the participants' knowledge or skills. Avoid being too overwhelming. Instead, focus on demonstrating the value and benefits they can gain from the additional product or service.

Provide Exclusive Discounts or Bonuses: Offer exclusive discounts, bonuses, or early bird pricing for the upsell or cross-sell offer to webinar participants. Create a sense of urgency and scarcity by emphasizing that the offer is only available for a limited time or to a limited number of participants. This can encourage immediate action and conversions.

Showcase Testimonials or Case Studies: Share testimonials or case studies highlighting the success stories of individuals or businesses that have benefited from the upsell or cross-sell offer. This social proof helps build credibility and trust, increasing the likelihood of participants taking advantage of the offer.

Create a Seamless User Experience: Ensure a seamless transition from the webinar to the upsell or cross-sell offer. Provide clear instructions on how participants can access the offer, whether it's through a dedicated webpage, a unique promo code, or a direct link. Make the purchasing process easy, intuitive, and secure.

Follow Up with Email Marketing: Follow up with participants after the webinar through email marketing. Send personalized emails that highlight the benefits of the upsell or cross-sell offer and reiterate the exclusive discounts or bonuses. Include compelling CTAs and links to the offer to drive conversions.

Offer Bundled Packages or Add-Ons: Consider creating bundled packages that combine the webinar content with the upsell or cross-sell offer. This can provide additional value and incentive for participants to make a purchase. Alternatively, offer add-ons or supplementary resources that enhance the learning experience and support the upsell or cross-sell offer.

Provide Ongoing Support and Value: Ensure that participants who take advantage of the upsell or cross-sell offer receive exceptional customer support, access to exclusive resources, or additional training materials. Delivering ongoing value strengthens customer satisfaction and increases the likelihood of repeat purchases or referrals.

Continuously Optimize and Refine: Monitor the performance of your upsell and cross-sell strategies by tracking conversion rates, revenue generated, and participant feedback. Analyze the effectiveness of different offers, pricing strategies, and marketing techniques. Make data-driven decisions to optimize your upselling and cross-selling efforts.

By incorporating upselling and cross-selling techniques into your webinars, you can generate additional revenue while providing valuable solutions to your audience. Remember to maintain transparency, focus on delivering value, and align the upsell or cross-sell offers with the needs and interests of your participants. With strategic upselling and cross-selling, your webinars can become a profitable income stream that enhances the overall participant experience.

5. **Membership or Subscription Model**: Create a membership or subscription model around your webinar content. Offer ongoing access to a library of recorded webinars, exclusive resources, or a community of like-minded individuals. Participants pay a recurring fee to gain continuous access to the valuable content and benefits you provide.

Making Money with Webinars through Membership or Subscription Model

Let's imagine you are an expert in personal development and regularly host webinars on topics such as goal setting, time management, and self-improvement. Here's an example of how you can make money with webinars through a membership or subscription model:

Develop a Membership Program: Create a membership program that offers exclusive benefits and access to a community of like-minded individuals seeking personal growth. Consider what additional value you can provide to members beyond your regular webinars, such as access to a private online forum, bonus resources, or monthly Q&A sessions.

Set a Subscription Fee: Determine a monthly or annual subscription fee that reflects the value of the membership program. Research similar programs in your industry to ensure your pricing is competitive and aligns with the perceived value you offer. Consider offering different subscription tiers with varying benefits to cater to different audience segments.

Highlight Membership Benefits: Clearly communicate the benefits of your membership program during your webinars and on your website. Emphasize the exclusive access to premium content, personalized support, networking opportunities, and ongoing education that members will receive. Showcase testimonials or success stories from existing members to demonstrate the value of the program.

Offer a Free Trial or Introductory Period: Attract potential members by offering a free trial or discounted introductory period. This allows individuals to experience the value of the membership program firsthand and encourages them to continue as paying members after the trial period ends. Ensure the trial period provides a sufficient taste of the benefits to entice conversion.

Create Member-Only Webinars: In addition to your regular webinars, host exclusive webinars or workshops specifically for members. These sessions can delve deeper into specific topics, provide advanced insights, or feature guest experts. This creates a sense of exclusivity and incentivizes non-members to join the membership program to access this premium content.

Foster Community Engagement: Encourage member engagement by creating a dedicated online community platform where members can connect, share experiences, and support each other. This can be a private forum, a social media group, or a designated membership website. Actively participate in the community, answer questions, and facilitate discussions to foster a vibrant and valuable community.

Continuously Add Value: Regularly provide new content and resources exclusively for members to keep them engaged and subscribed. This can include member-only articles, downloadable guides, video tutorials, or access to your archived webinar library. Consider conducting surveys or polls to gather feedback and tailor your offerings to meet the evolving needs of your members.

Retain Members through Renewal Incentives: Implement renewal incentives to encourage members to continue their subscription. Offer discounted renewal rates, bonuses, or exclusive offers to reward loyalty. Remind members of the value they have received and highlight upcoming content or benefits to entice them to renew.

Promote the Membership Program: Promote your membership program through various marketing channels. Leverage your email list, social media platforms, website, and webinars to highlight the benefits and value of becoming a member. Collaborate with influencers or affiliates who can promote your membership program to their respective audiences.

Provide Excellent Customer Support: Deliver exceptional customer support to your members. Respond promptly to inquiries, address concerns, and actively seek feedback to continuously improve the membership experience. Building strong relationships and a reputation for outstanding support will increase member satisfaction and retention.

By implementing a membership or subscription model for your webinars, you can create a recurring revenue stream while providing ongoing value and support to your audience. Remember to continuously assess member satisfaction, refine your offerings, and nurture your community to ensure long-term success. With a thriving membership program, your webinars can become a profitable and impactful part of your business.

6. **Product or Service Launches**: Use webinars to launch new products, services, or programs. Build anticipation and excitement around your offering and leverage the webinar as a platform to demonstrate its value and benefits. Incorporate a call-to-action for participants to make a purchase or sign up for your offering during or after the webinar.

Example: Using Webinars to Launch New Products, Services, or Programs

Let's imagine you are an entrepreneur in the fitness industry and are about to launch a new online fitness program. Here's an example of how you can use webinars to successfully launch your new product:

Pre-Launch Webinar: Host a pre-launch webinar to generate excitement and anticipation for your upcoming fitness program. Promote the webinar through your email list, social media channels, and website, inviting your audience to join and learn about the program's benefits and features.

Present the Program: During the webinar, introduce your new fitness program in detail. Highlight its unique selling points, such as the specific workout routines, meal plans, or personalized coaching it offers. Explain how it addresses your audience's fitness goals, challenges, or pain points.

Demonstrate Value: Showcase the value of your program by providing a taste of what participants can expect. Conduct a mini-workout session, offer nutrition tips, or share success stories from individuals who have already tested the program. This firsthand experience will demonstrate the effectiveness of your offering.

Exclusive Offer: Create a sense of urgency and exclusivity by offering a limited-time, special launch discount or bonus for webinar attendees. Encourage them to sign up for the program during the webinar to take advantage of the exclusive offer. Provide a clear call-to-action with a link or button directing them to the registration page.

Q&A Session: Allocate time for a Q&A session during the webinar, allowing participants to ask questions about the program. Address concerns, provide clarifications, and highlight the support and resources available to participants. This interactive session builds trust and helps participants make informed decisions about joining the program.

Follow-Up Email: After the webinar, send a follow-up email to all attendees. Include a recording of the webinar for those who couldn't attend, along with a recap of the program's features and benefits. Remind them of the exclusive offer and encourage them to take action before the deadline.

Webinar Replay: Consider hosting a replay of the webinar for those who missed the live session. Promote the replay through your email list and social media channels, allowing interested individuals to access the content and still benefit from the exclusive launch offer.

Limited-Time Offer Reminders: Send reminder emails as the deadline for the special launch offer approaches. Create a sense of urgency by emphasizing the limited availability of the discount or bonus. Use persuasive language to motivate potential customers to take action before the offer expires.

Collaborate with Influencers: Reach out to fitness influencers or industry experts and invite them to participate in the webinar or share the launch with their audiences. Collaborating with influencers can expand your reach and lend credibility to your new program, attracting more potential customers.

Post-Launch Support: Once the program launches, provide ongoing support and engagement to your participants. Conduct regular check-ins, offer additional resources, and create a community where participants can connect and share their progress. This ongoing support fosters loyalty and encourages referrals for future program launches.

By leveraging webinars as part of your launch strategy, you can create buzz, engage your audience, and drive conversions for your new products, services, or programs. Remember to communicate the value of your offering, provide exclusive launch incentives, and deliver exceptional support to ensure a successful launch.

7. **Consulting or Coaching Services:** Position yourself as an expert in your field and offer consulting or coaching services related to your webinar topic. Use webinars to showcase your expertise and build trust with participants. Offer personalized services to individuals or businesses seeking guidance or support beyond the webinar content.

Example: Making Money with Webinars through Consulting or Coaching Services

Let's imagine you are a marketing consultant with extensive experience in digital marketing strategies. You want to leverage webinars to attract clients and generate income through consulting services. Here's an example of how you can make money with webinars through consulting or coaching services:

Choose a Specific Webinar Topic: Select a webinar topic that highlights your expertise and addresses a pressing challenge faced by your target audience. For instance, you could host a webinar on "Effective Strategies to Boost Online Visibility and Drive Conversions."

Promote the Webinar: Utilize your email list, social media channels, and professional networks to promote the webinar. Create visually appealing graphics and compelling copy to capture the attention of potential attendees. Emphasize the value they will gain from attending your webinar.

Provide Valuable Content: During the webinar, share valuable insights, practical tips, and real-world examples that demonstrate your expertise. Showcase your in-depth knowledge of digital marketing and how it can benefit businesses seeking to improve their online presence.

Offer a Consultation Opportunity: Towards the end of the webinar, invite attendees to schedule a one-on-one consultation or coaching session with you. Clearly explain the benefits of the personalized advice and guidance they will receive during the session.

Create an Irresistible Consultation Offer: Offer an exclusive, limited-time discount or bonus for those who sign up for a consultation during the webinar. Provide a direct link or a dedicated landing page where attendees can book their consultation at the special rate.

Q&A Session: Include a Q&A session at the end of the webinar, allowing attendees to ask specific questions related to their businesses. This interactive engagement builds trust and confidence in your expertise, increasing the likelihood of consultation sign-ups.

Follow-Up Email: After the webinar, send a follow-up email to all attendees, whether they signed up for the consultation or not. Include a recording of the webinar, a summary of key points, and a reminder of the consultation offer. Encourage them to take advantage of the limited-time discount before it expires.

Provide Value During Consultations: During the consultation sessions, focus on providing tailored advice and solutions based on each client's unique needs. Demonstrate your ability to understand their challenges and offer actionable strategies to overcome them.

Offer Package Deals: Consider offering package deals for multiple coaching or consulting sessions. Package deals can provide added value to clients and encourage them to commit to a longer-term engagement with you.

Request Testimonials and Referrals: Request testimonials from satisfied clients and seek their permission to share these testimonials on your website or marketing materials. Additionally, encourage clients to refer you to their networks if they find value in your services. Word-of-mouth referrals can be a powerful source of new clients.

By using webinars to showcase your expertise and offering personalized consulting or coaching services, you can attract clients and monetize your knowledge effectively. Remember to continuously provide value, offer exclusive incentives, and nurture relationships with your clients for repeat business and referrals.

8. **Repurposing Content**: Repurpose your webinar content into other formats, such as e-books, online courses, or digital downloads. Package and sell these materials as standalone products, providing additional value and revenue streams.

Example: Making Money with Webinars through Repurposing Content

Let's imagine you are a business strategist who regularly hosts webinars on various topics related to entrepreneurship and leadership. Here's an example of how you can make money with webinars by repurposing your webinar content into other formats and selling them as standalone products:

Host Informative Webinars: Conduct engaging and informative webinars on topics relevant to your target audience, such as "Strategies for Building a Successful Online Business" or "Effective Leadership Techniques for Team Growth."

Record and Save Webinars: Record your webinars to preserve the valuable content. Ensure the recordings have high-quality audio and video to maintain professionalism and enhance the user experience.

Transcribe Webinar Content: Transcribe the webinar content into written format, creating a text-based document of the entire webinar content, including the presentation slides and Q&A sessions.

Create E-Books: Compile the transcribed content and additional insights into comprehensive e-books. Organize the e-books into chapters or sections for easy navigation and readability. Include visual elements, infographics, and illustrations to enhance the content.

Design Online Courses: Use your webinar recordings and e-book content as a foundation to design in-depth online courses. Divide the content into modules or lessons, add quizzes or assignments for interactive learning, and create video lectures or presentations to supplement the written material.

Develop Digital Downloads: Extract key insights, actionable tips, or templates from your webinar content to create downloadable resources. Offer checklists, planning guides, templates, or workbooks that your audience can use to implement the strategies discussed in the webinars.

Package and Price Products: Package your e-books, online courses, and digital downloads as standalone products. Offer them individually or create bundles that provide additional value at a discounted rate. Determine competitive pricing based on the quality and depth of the content.

Create a Sales Funnel: Integrate your standalone products into a sales funnel. Use your webinars to drive awareness and interest in your products, and provide links to purchase the products during or after the webinar. Offer exclusive discounts or bonuses to webinar attendees to encourage immediate purchases.

Market Your Products: Promote your standalone products through various marketing channels. Leverage your email list, social media platforms, blog posts, and webinars to reach your target audience. Share testimonials or reviews from satisfied customers to build trust and credibility.

Offer Upsells and Cross-Sells: During the sales process, consider offering upsells or cross-sells to encourage customers to explore additional products or higher-priced packages. For instance, after purchasing an e-book, offer a discounted rate for enrolling in the complete online course.

By repurposing your webinar content into other formats and selling them as standalone products, you can generate additional revenue streams while providing valuable resources to your audience. Remember to maintain the quality of your content, continuously update and improve your products, and adapt your offerings based on customer feedback and market demand. With a strategic approach, you can turn your webinars into a profitable and sustainable business venture.

9. **Corporate Sponsorship or Training**: Approach companies or organizations that may benefit from your expertise and offer to conduct customized webinars or training sessions for their employees or stakeholders. Tailor the content to their specific needs and negotiate a fee or sponsorship arrangement.

Example: Making Money with Webinars through Corporate Sponsorship or Training

Let's imagine you are an expert in workplace productivity and time management. You have a successful track record of hosting webinars on these topics and want to explore opportunities for corporate sponsorship or training. Here's an example of how you can make money with webinars through corporate sponsorship or training:

Showcase Expertise through Webinars: Continue hosting webinars on workplace productivity and time management, providing valuable insights, tips, and actionable strategies for individuals and businesses.

Target Corporate Audiences: Focus on attracting a corporate audience for your webinars. Highlight the benefits of improved productivity and time management for businesses, such as increased efficiency, reduced costs, and improved employee satisfaction.

Reach Out to Potential Sponsors: Identify companies or organizations that align with your expertise and target audience. Reach out to their marketing or training departments to propose corporate sponsorship for your webinars. Emphasize the value their brand can gain from associating with your webinars and reaching a relevant audience.

Create Sponsorship Packages: Develop sponsorship packages that outline the benefits and exposure sponsors will receive during your webinars. This could include logo placement on webinar slides, verbal recognition during the webinar, promotional mentions in marketing materials, and access to attendee data for follow-up.

Tailor Webinars for Corporate Training: Offer customized webinars specifically designed for corporate training purposes. Develop webinar content that addresses specific productivity and time management challenges faced by businesses and their employees.

Highlight Real-World Solutions: Incorporate case studies or success stories of companies that have implemented your productivity strategies with positive outcomes. Demonstrate how your training can bring tangible results to corporate teams.

Provide Interactive Training: Incorporate interactive elements into your corporate training webinars, such as polls, quizzes, and group discussions. This engagement fosters a more immersive learning experience and reinforces the retention of key concepts.

Offer Corporate Training Packages: Develop comprehensive corporate training packages that include multiple webinars, personalized coaching sessions, and post-webinar support. Package your offerings to cater to the needs of different businesses and industries.

Host Exclusive Webinars for Corporate Clients: Offer exclusive webinars for corporate clients, tailored to their specific needs and challenges. Consider hosting private webinars for individual companies or conducting company-wide training sessions.

Measure Training Impact: Follow up with corporate clients after the webinars to assess the impact of the training on their productivity and time management. Request feedback and testimonials that can be used to attract more corporate clients in the future.

By exploring corporate sponsorship and training opportunities for your webinars, you can generate revenue while providing valuable expertise and training to businesses. Remember to tailor your content and offerings to the needs of corporate audiences, showcase the value of your expertise, and maintain professional relationships with your sponsors and clients. With the right approach, your webinars can become a lucrative revenue stream and a sought-after training solution for corporate clients.

10. **Donations or Crowdfunding**: If you provide valuable content that resonates with your audience, you can consider accepting voluntary donations or setting up a crowdfunding campaign to support your webinar efforts. This approach works particularly well if you provide educational or nonprofit-related webinars.

Example: Making Money with Webinars through Donations or Crowdfunding

Let's imagine you are a passionate environmental activist with a strong following on social media. You regularly host webinars on various environmental issues and conservation efforts. Here's an example of how you can make money with webinars through donations or crowdfunding:

Engage Your Audience: Continue hosting informative webinars on environmental topics, raising awareness about pressing issues such as climate change, wildlife conservation, and sustainable practices.

Build a Dedicated Community: Foster a dedicated community of environmentally-conscious individuals who are passionate about making a positive impact on the planet. Utilize social media, email newsletters, and your website to nurture and expand your audience.

Choose a Fundraising Cause: Select a specific environmental cause or project that requires funding. For instance, you could aim to raise funds for tree-planting initiatives, wildlife rehabilitation centers, or environmental education programs.

Set Up a Crowdfunding Campaign: Create a crowdfunding campaign on a reputable platform such as Kickstarter, Indiegogo, or GoFundMe. Clearly explain your fundraising goal, the purpose of the campaign, and how the donations will contribute to the chosen environmental cause.

Leverage Webinars for Fundraising: Host webinars dedicated to fundraising for the selected cause. During these webinars, share compelling stories, visual presentations, and real-life examples to illustrate the importance and impact of the cause. Emphasize how every contribution, no matter the size, can make a difference.

Offer Incentives: Encourage donations by offering incentives for various contribution levels. For instance, donors who contribute a certain amount could receive exclusive access to additional webinars, eco-friendly merchandise, or personalized thank-you messages.

Collaborate with Environmental Experts: Invite environmental experts, scientists, or activists to co-host webinars with you. Their involvement can lend credibility to your fundraising efforts and attract a broader audience.

Promote the Crowdfunding Campaign: Utilize all available marketing channels to promote your crowdfunding campaign. Share links to the campaign on social media, in your email newsletters, and during your webinars. Encourage your audience to share the campaign with their networks as well.

Offer Transparency and Updates: Be transparent with your audience about the progress of the crowdfunding campaign. Regularly update your supporters on the funds raised and how they will be utilized for the environmental cause.

Express Gratitude: Show genuine appreciation to all donors and supporters. Acknowledge their contributions during your webinars, on your website, and through personalized thank-you messages. Expressing gratitude strengthens the connection between you and your audience.

By leveraging webinars for fundraising efforts, you can engage your audience in meaningful environmental causes and make a positive impact on the planet. Remember to remain passionate and authentic in your mission, inspire others to join your cause, and maintain open communication with your supporters. With their support and contributions, your webinars can be a catalyst for positive change and help fund important environmental initiatives.

Remember to create high-quality, valuable webinar content that meets the needs and interests of your target audience. Building a reputation for providing exceptional content will help you attract participants and generate revenue from your webinars.

11. **Through YouTube**: Making money with webinars through YouTube can be achieved through several strategies that leverage the platform's features and audience reach. Here are some ways to monetize webinars on YouTube:
Create Engaging Webinar Content: Host informative and engaging webinars on topics that resonate with your target audience. Offer valuable insights, practical tips, and actionable advice to attract and retain viewers.

Enable YouTube Monetization: Join the YouTube Partner Program to monetize your content through ads. Once your channel meets the eligibility criteria, you can enable ads on your videos and earn revenue based on ad views and clicks.

Promote Products or Services: During your webinars, promote relevant products, services, or online courses that you offer. Include affiliate links or links to your website where viewers can make purchases or sign up for your offerings.

Leverage YouTube Sponsorships: As your channel grows in popularity, you may attract sponsorships from brands or companies that want to collaborate with you. These sponsorships could include sponsored segments within your webinars or shout-outs for products or services.

Offer Exclusive Content with Memberships: Utilize YouTube's channel membership feature to offer exclusive content to paying members. You can host members-only webinars, behind-the-scenes content, or Q&A sessions for your loyal subscribers.

Promote Webinars on Social Media: Extend the reach of your webinars by promoting them on other social media platforms, such as Instagram, Twitter, or

Facebook. This can drive more viewers to your YouTube channel and increase engagement.

Collaborate with Other YouTubers: Collaborate with other content creators or influencers in your niche to co-host webinars or participate in joint projects. This cross-promotion can introduce your channel to new audiences and increase your subscriber base.

Use YouTube Super Chat: Enable the Super Chat feature during live webinars, allowing viewers to purchase highlighted messages that stand out in the chat. This provides an additional revenue stream during live sessions.

Offer Paid Webinars or Workshops: Host special, in-depth webinars or workshops that require viewers to pay a fee for access. Promote these paid webinars through your regular content and social media channels.

Repurpose Webinar Content: Repurpose your webinar content into shorter clips, highlights, or compilations that appeal to different audiences. This increases the visibility of your content and can attract more viewers to your channel.

Remember that building a successful YouTube channel and making money through webinars takes time, consistency, and dedication. Focus on providing value to your viewers, engaging with your audience, and optimizing your content for discoverability on YouTube. As your channel grows and gains a loyal following, you can explore various monetization options to generate income from your webinars and overall content.

Example

Let's consider an example of how a fitness and nutrition expert can make money with webinars through YouTube:

Example: Fitness and Nutrition Webinars on YouTube

Create Engaging Webinar Content: The fitness and nutrition expert hosts regular webinars on their YouTube channel, covering topics such as "Effective Home Workouts," "Healthy Meal Planning for Weight Loss," and "Boosting Immunity with Nutrient-Rich Foods."

Enable YouTube Monetization: The expert joins the YouTube Partner Program, which allows them to enable ads on their webinar videos. As their channel gains views and subscribers, they start earning revenue from ad views and clicks.

Promote Products or Services: During their webinars, the expert promotes their fitness and nutrition e-books, online courses, and workout programs. They include links to their website in the video descriptions, directing viewers to purchase these offerings.

Leverage YouTube Sponsorships: As the fitness and nutrition expert's channel grows, they attract sponsorships from health and wellness brands. These sponsorships involve promoting the brands' products or services within their webinars, and they receive compensation for these collaborations.

Offer Exclusive Content with Memberships: The expert offers a channel membership program where subscribers can become members and gain access to exclusive content. They host monthly members-only webinars, providing personalized fitness and nutrition advice.

Promote Webinars on Social Media: The expert shares highlights and clips from their webinars on platforms like Instagram, Twitter, and Facebook. They use catchy captions and hashtags to attract viewers to their YouTube channel.

Collaborate with Other YouTubers: The fitness and nutrition expert collaborates with other fitness influencers and health experts. They co-host webinars or participate in joint Q&A sessions, introducing each other's audiences to new content.

Use YouTube Super Chat: During their live webinars, the expert enables Super Chat, allowing viewers to purchase highlighted messages. This not only increases engagement but also provides additional revenue during live sessions.

Offer Paid Webinars or Workshops: Occasionally, the expert hosts paid webinars or workshops with in-depth topics like "Customized Meal Plans for Specific Goals" or "Advanced Fitness Techniques." Viewers pay a fee to access these specialized sessions.

Repurpose Webinar Content: The expert repurposes their webinar content into short workout routines, recipe tutorials, and health tips. They create compilation videos or "best of" lists to attract new viewers to their channel.

Over time, the fitness and nutrition expert's YouTube channel grows in popularity and attracts a large and engaged audience. By effectively leveraging YouTube's monetization features, promoting their products and services, and collaborating with other influencers, they establish multiple revenue streams through their webinars and content. As their channel becomes a trusted source of fitness and nutrition advice, they continue to generate income while helping viewers achieve their health and wellness goals.

12. **Continuity Programs**: Offer continuity programs or ongoing memberships where participants pay a recurring fee to receive access to a series of webinars or exclusive content on a regular basis. This provides a steady stream of revenue and fosters long-term relationships with your audience.

Example: Making Money with Webinars through Continuity Programs or Ongoing Memberships

Let's imagine you are a professional life coach with expertise in personal development and mental well-being. You want to create a continuity program that offers ongoing value to your clients through a series of webinars and exclusive content. Here's an example of how you can make money with webinars through continuity programs or ongoing memberships:

Define Your Target Audience: Identify your target audience, such as individuals seeking personal growth, stress management, or work-life balance. Understand their needs and pain points to tailor your webinar content accordingly.

Plan a Series of Webinars: Develop a series of webinars that cover a range of topics relevant to your audience. For instance, you could have webinars on goal setting, overcoming limiting beliefs, building resilience, and cultivating mindfulness.

Create a Membership Website: Set up a membership website where participants can subscribe to access the webinars and exclusive content. Offer different membership tiers with varying levels of access, benefits, and pricing.

Offer Exclusive Content: In addition to webinars, provide exclusive content such as downloadable resources, guided meditations, and workbooks that complement the webinar topics. This added value encourages participants to join and remain in the membership program.

Set a Recurring Fee: Determine a recurring monthly or annual fee for the membership program based on the level of access and value provided. Price your memberships competitively to attract and retain participants.

Launch the Continuity Program: Launch the continuity program through a webinar or a series of webinars. Promote the program through your email list, social media channels, and other marketing efforts.

Host Regular Webinars: Schedule regular webinars as part of the continuity program. Hold webinars on a weekly or monthly basis, depending on your chosen membership structure. Maintain consistency to keep participants engaged.

Interact and Engage: Encourage interaction and engagement during the webinars. Incorporate Q&A sessions, polls, and interactive exercises to foster a sense of community among the members.

Provide Ongoing Support: Offer ongoing support to your members through the membership website or private community forums. Respond to their questions, provide feedback, and offer additional resources as needed.

Retain and Renew: Focus on member retention by continuously delivering valuable content, monitoring feedback, and addressing any concerns promptly. Encourage members to renew their memberships by offering incentives, discounts, or exclusive offers for loyal participants.

By offering a continuity program with ongoing webinars and exclusive content, you can create a sustainable and profitable income stream while providing continuous value to your audience. Remember to deliver high-quality webinars, nurture your community, and regularly assess and improve the membership program based on participant feedback. With a well-structured continuity program, you can build long-term relationships with your clients and create a thriving online community.

13. **Joint Ventures and Co-hosting**: Collaborate with other experts or influencers in your industry to co-host webinars. This allows you to leverage each other's audience and expertise, and potentially generate more registrations and revenue through shared promotions or revenue-sharing arrangements.

Example: Making Money with Webinars through Collaboration with Industry Experts

Let's imagine you are a digital marketing specialist with expertise in social media strategies. You want to leverage webinars to increase your reach and generate income. Here's an example of how you can make money with webinars through collaboration with other experts or influencers in your industry:

Identify Potential Collaborators: Research and identify other experts or influencers in the digital marketing industry who complement your expertise. Look for individuals with a significant following or expertise in related areas, such as content marketing or email marketing.

Reach Out to Collaborators: Reach out to your potential collaborators through email or social media. Introduce yourself, explain your webinar concept, and highlight the benefits of co-hosting a webinar together. Emphasize how both of you can leverage each other's audiences to increase visibility and engagement.

Plan a Joint Webinar Topic: Collaborate with your chosen expert to choose a webinar topic that aligns with both your audiences and addresses a specific pain point or challenge. For example, you could co-host a webinar on "Powerful Social Media Strategies to Boost Your Online Presence."

Split the Workload: Divide the webinar preparation and presentation responsibilities between you and your collaborator. Assign specific sections or topics to each person based on their expertise and interest.

Promote the Webinar Together: Coordinate your marketing efforts with your collaborator to promote the webinar to both of your audiences. Use email lists, social media platforms, and other marketing channels to reach a broader audience.

Offer Joint Incentives: Create joint incentives for participants to attend the webinar. This could include exclusive resources, discounts on your respective products or services, or access to a private community.

Leverage Cross-Promotion: Cross-promote each other's products, services, or webinars during the co-hosted event. Mention any special offers or deals available to attendees for a limited time.

Provide Value and Engagement: During the webinar, ensure both you and your collaborator deliver valuable insights and actionable tips. Encourage audience engagement through polls, Q&A sessions, and interactive discussions.

Capture Leads: Offer a lead capture form or a call-to-action at the end of the webinar to capture attendees' contact information. This enables you to follow up with potential leads and nurture them further.

Offer Post-Webinar Products or Services: After the webinar, collaborate on additional products or services that cater to the shared interests of your audiences.

For example, you could offer a joint online course or a bundle of your digital marketing services.

By collaborating with other experts or influencers in your industry to co-host webinars, you can tap into new audiences, increase your credibility, and generate revenue through joint marketing efforts. Focus on delivering value to the attendees and building a mutually beneficial partnership with your collaborators. With strategic collaboration, your webinars can become a profitable source of income and business growth.

14. **Certification or Accreditation Programs**: Develop and offer certification or accreditation programs through your webinars. Participants who successfully complete the program and meet the requirements receive a recognized certification or accreditation, which can increase the perceived value and justify a higher price point.

Example: Making Money Online through Certification or Accreditation Programs

Let's imagine you are a professional coach specializing in leadership development. You have a successful track record of helping individuals and organizations enhance their leadership skills. Here's an example of how you can make money online through certification or accreditation programs:

Establish Your Expertise: Build a strong online presence by sharing valuable content related to leadership development through blog posts, social media, and webinars. Establish yourself as a credible authority in your field.

Develop a Comprehensive Leadership Certification Program: Create a detailed leadership certification program that covers essential leadership competencies and skills. Plan the program curriculum to be comprehensive and actionable, providing valuable insights and practical training.

Design a Structured Online Course: Transform your certification program into a structured online course. Use a combination of video lectures, interactive exercises, quizzes, and downloadable resources to engage learners and facilitate learning.

Set a Certification Fee: Determine a reasonable certification fee that reflects the value of your program. Consider pricing options, such as a one-time payment or a recurring subscription for ongoing access to program updates and resources.

Offer Additional Support and Resources: Enhance the value of your certification program by providing additional support, such as live Q&A sessions, personalized coaching, and access to a private community or forum for networking and peer support.

Attract Potential Learners: Promote your certification program through various marketing channels, including your website, email newsletters, social media platforms, and collaborations with industry influencers. Highlight the career and personal development benefits of obtaining your certification.

Provide Recognition and Accreditation: Offer an official certification or accreditation upon successful completion of the program. Emphasize the credibility and recognition that learners will gain within their organizations or industries by earning your certification.

Encourage Corporate Sponsorship: Reach out to corporations and organizations that value leadership development. Offer corporate sponsorship packages for groups of employees to enroll in your certification program. Highlight the positive impact on leadership effectiveness within their workforce.

Create Upsell Opportunities: Offer advanced or specialized certification tracks for learners who complete the initial certification program. Upsell these additional tracks to provide ongoing learning and development opportunities.

Gather Testimonials and Success Stories: Collect testimonials and success stories from certified individuals who have benefited from your program. Showcase these positive experiences on your website and marketing materials to build trust and credibility with potential learners.

By offering a high-quality leadership certification program online, you can attract learners seeking professional development opportunities and generate revenue through course enrollment and certification fees. Continuously update and improve your program based on learner feedback and market demands to ensure it remains relevant and valuable. As your certification program gains recognition and positive reviews, it can become a lucrative income stream while making a positive impact on the professional growth of your learners.

15. **Premium Add-ons or Resources**: Offer premium add-ons or resources to enhance the webinar experience. This could include access to downloadable

materials, worksheets, templates, or exclusive tools that complement the webinar content. Participants can purchase these additional resources at an extra cost.

Example: Making Money Online through Premium Add-ons or Resources

Let's imagine you are a professional graphic designer who offers online courses on graphic design principles and techniques. Here's an example of how you can make money online through premium add-ons or resources:

Offer Comprehensive Online Courses: Develop in-depth online courses on various aspects of graphic design, such as typography, logo design, or digital illustration. Ensure that your courses are well-structured, engaging, and packed with valuable content.

Identify Additional Needs: Identify specific areas within your courses where learners may require additional resources or tools to enhance their learning experience. For example, learners may need access to high-quality stock images, design templates, or exclusive design assets.

Create Premium Add-ons: Develop premium add-ons or resources that complement your online courses. This could include a bundle of design templates, exclusive graphic design asset packs, or access to a private library of stock images curated by you.

Package Premium Resources: Package the premium add-ons as part of a "Design Toolkit" or "Designer's Resource Pack." Offer these resources as optional upgrades or add-ons to your online courses, allowing learners to enhance their skills with valuable assets.

Set a Premium Add-on Price: Determine a reasonable price for the premium resources, considering the value they provide to learners and the level of exclusivity. Offer the premium add-ons at a price point that encourages learners to see them as valuable investments in their professional growth.

Promote the Premium Add-ons: Promote the premium add-ons through your course platform, email newsletters, and social media channels. Highlight the benefits and unique features of these resources, emphasizing how they can help learners save time and enhance their design projects.

Upsell and Bundle Options: Create upsell opportunities by offering bundled packages that include both the online course and the premium add-ons at a discounted rate. Encourage learners to take advantage of the bundled options to maximize their learning experience.

Offer Limited-Time Deals: Occasionally, offer limited-time deals or discounts on the premium add-ons to create a sense of urgency among your audience. This can prompt learners to make a purchasing decision sooner rather than later.

Provide Excellent Customer Support: Offer exceptional customer support to users who purchase the premium add-ons. Address any inquiries or concerns promptly, and ensure that learners have a positive experience with the resources.

Continuously Update and Improve: Regularly update and improve your premium add-ons to keep them relevant and valuable to your learners. Consider gathering feedback from users and incorporating their suggestions to enhance the resources further.

By offering premium add-ons or resources that complement your online courses, you can create an additional revenue stream while providing valuable tools and assets to your learners. Focus on delivering high-quality content and staying attuned to the needs of your audience to ensure the success of your premium offerings. As your reputation for providing valuable resources grows, so will the potential for increased revenue and customer loyalty.

16. **Corporate Training and Workshops**: Approach companies or organizations and offer customized webinars as part of their training and development programs. Tailor the content to their specific needs and goals, and negotiate a fee for conducting the webinar or providing ongoing training sessions.

Example: Making Money with Webinars through Corporate Training and Workshops

Let's imagine you are a communication skills expert with a proven track record in delivering effective corporate training and workshops. Here's an example of how you can make money with webinars by offering corporate training and workshops:

Identify Target Industries: Determine the industries or businesses that can benefit from communication skills training. Target sectors like finance, healthcare, or technology, where effective communication is crucial for success.

Design a Customizable Training Program: Develop a comprehensive communication skills training program that addresses common challenges in corporate environments. Include modules on effective presentations, conflict resolution, active listening, and professional writing.

Promote Webinar Training Sessions: Promote your communication skills training program through targeted marketing efforts. Utilize email outreach, social media, and collaborations with industry influencers to attract corporate clients.

Offer Customizable Workshops: Customize your training program based on the specific needs of each corporate client. Tailor the content and duration of the workshop to address their communication challenges and objectives.

Set Competitive Pricing: Determine competitive pricing for your corporate training webinars and workshops. Consider factors such as the program's scope, duration, and level of customization.

Engage Corporate HR and L&D Departments: Build relationships with corporate HR and Learning & Development (L&D) departments. Offer insights on how your training program can enhance their employees' communication skills and overall productivity.

Provide Interactive Webinars: Conduct interactive webinars that include live presentations, group activities, role-playing exercises, and Q&A sessions. Engaging activities encourage active participation and better retention of learning.

Showcase Past Successes: Highlight success stories and positive feedback from previous corporate clients. Share testimonials and case studies that demonstrate the tangible benefits of your communication skills training.

Offer Follow-Up Support: Provide post-webinar support to corporate clients, such as access to additional resources, one-on-one coaching sessions, or follow-up webinars to reinforce the learning.

Seek Repeat Business and Referrals: Aim to establish long-term relationships with corporate clients. Encourage repeat business and referrals by consistently delivering high-quality training sessions that bring tangible improvements to their teams.

Scale through On-Demand Webinars: Consider offering on-demand versions of your communication skills training webinars. This allows corporate clients to access the training at their convenience, expanding your reach and revenue potential.

Collaborate with Corporate Trainers: Collaborate with other corporate trainers or experts to offer comprehensive training programs that combine your communication skills expertise with other relevant skills, such as leadership or team-building.

By offering high-quality and results-driven communication skills training through webinars and workshops, you can attract corporate clients seeking to invest in their employees' professional development. Continuous improvement of your training program based on client feedback will contribute to building a strong reputation and increasing your revenue as you become a sought-after corporate training expert.

17. **Sponsored Content or Product Placement:** Incorporate sponsored content or product placement within your webinar. This involves featuring or promoting specific brands, products, or services during the webinar in exchange for financial compensation or other forms of support.

Example: Making Money with Webinars through Sponsored Content and Product Placement

Let's imagine you are a popular fitness influencer known for hosting webinars on health and wellness topics. Here's an example of how you can make money with webinars through sponsored content and product placement:

Establish a Niche: Focus on a specific niche within the health and wellness industry. For instance, you could specialize in home workouts, healthy meal planning, or mindfulness practices.

Build a Strong Audience: Grow your webinar audience through engaging content, social media presence, and collaborations with other health influencers. A sizable and engaged audience will attract potential sponsors.

Research Potential Sponsors: Identify companies or brands that align with your niche and target audience. Look for health and wellness products or services that complement the topics you cover in your webinars.

Create Sponsored Content Opportunities: Develop various sponsorship packages that offer brands opportunities to be featured in your webinars. This could include sponsored segments, product placements, or mentions in your webinar scripts.

Highlight Sponsor Benefits: Clearly outline the benefits sponsors will receive by partnering with you. Emphasize the reach and engagement of your audience, as well as the opportunity to showcase their products or services to a targeted demographic.

Showcase Sponsored Products: During your webinars, seamlessly incorporate sponsored products or services into your content. For example, if you are discussing healthy meal planning, you could feature a sponsored meal delivery service.

Include Sponsor Messages: Integrate sponsored messages or calls-to-action into your webinar scripts. Mention exclusive offers or discounts that sponsors are providing to your audience.

Promote Sponsored Webinars: Use your marketing channels, such as email newsletters and social media, to promote your sponsored webinars. Make sure to highlight the involvement of the sponsoring brands in your promotional materials.

Measure and Report Results: Provide sponsors with data and insights on the impact of their sponsorship, such as webinar attendance, engagement rates, and click-throughs to their websites. This data will demonstrate the value of the partnership.

Cultivate Long-Term Partnerships: Foster long-term relationships with sponsors by delivering value and achieving positive results. Repeat collaborations with satisfied sponsors can lead to ongoing revenue streams.

Disclose Sponsored Content: Ensure transparency with your audience by clearly disclosing sponsored content or product placements during your webinars. This builds trust and credibility with your viewers.

Explore Affiliate Partnerships: In addition to sponsored content, consider joining affiliate programs for products or services that align with your niche. Promote affiliate products during your webinars and earn commissions for each sale generated through your referrals.

By incorporating sponsored content and product placement in your webinars, you can monetize your influence and expertise in the health and wellness industry. Remember to strike a balance between sponsored content and valuable information for your audience, ensuring that your webinars remain engaging and authentic. With successful partnerships, you can create a steady stream of income while providing your audience with valuable insights and access to relevant products or services.

18. **Premium Support or Coaching Packages**: Offer premium support or coaching packages that provide participants with additional one-on-one guidance or personalized assistance related to the webinar topic. This can include personalized consultations, coaching calls, or email support for a premium fee.

19. **Pay-per-View or On-Demand Webinars**: Record and package your webinars as on-demand content that participants can access for a fee. Alternatively, you can offer pay-per-view options where participants pay a one-time fee to watch a specific webinar of their choice.

20. **Ad Revenue**: If your webinar platform allows it, you can generate revenue by incorporating advertisements or sponsored messages during your webinars. This can be especially effective if you have a large and engaged audience.

21. **Exclusive Access or Early Bird Pricing**: Provide exclusive access or early bird pricing for future webinars to participants who have attended previous paid webinars. This rewards their loyalty and encourages repeat attendance, generating additional revenue.

Remember to always prioritize delivering value to your participants and maintaining the quality of your content. Continuously assess and refine your monetization strategies based on feedback and the needs of your target audience.

22. **Affiliate Partnerships:** Collaborate with relevant affiliates who can promote your webinars to their audience in exchange for a commission on each sale or registration they generate. This allows you to leverage their existing network and tap into new potential participants.

23. **Exclusive Webinar Bundles or Packages:** Create bundled offerings that include multiple webinars or a combination of webinars, digital products, or services at a discounted price. This encourages participants to purchase multiple offerings together, increasing the average transaction value.

24. **Customized Sponsorship Opportunities**: Offer customized sponsorship opportunities where companies or brands can sponsor specific segments or themes within your webinar. This can include logo placement, sponsored shout-outs, or dedicated promotional segments.

25. **Premium Event Upgrades**: If you host live events or conferences, offer premium event upgrades that include access to exclusive webinars, VIP sessions, networking opportunities, or additional resources. Participants can choose to upgrade their event experience for an additional fee.

26. **White Label Webinars**: Provide white label webinar services where you offer your webinar platform and expertise as a branded solution to other businesses or organizations. They can host their own webinars using your platform, paying a fee for the service.

27. **Licensing or Selling Webinar Content:** Consider licensing or selling the rights to your webinar content to other organizations, training providers, or educational institutions. They can use your content as part of their own training programs or distribute it to their audience for a fee.

28. **Premium Group Coaching or Mastermind Programs**: Offer premium group coaching or mastermind programs that include a series of webinars along with coaching calls, group discussions, and additional resources. Participants pay a higher fee for the extended program and personalized support.

29. **Workshop or Training Materials**: Package your webinar content into comprehensive workshop or training materials, such as physical workbooks, manuals, or online courses. These materials can be sold as standalone products to participants who want to dive deeper into the webinar content.

30. **Sponsored Surveys or Market Research**: Conduct surveys or market research during your webinars and offer sponsorship opportunities to companies interested in collecting data or insights from your audience. This allows you to monetize the data you collect while providing value to sponsors.

31. **Membership or Affiliate Programs**: Create a membership program or affiliate program where participants can join for a recurring fee or earn commissions by referring others to your webinars. This builds a community and incentivizes participants to actively promote your webinars.

Remember to choose monetization strategies that align with your audience's preferences and needs. Regularly evaluate and refine your approach based on participant feedback and market trends to optimize your webinar monetization efforts.

32. **Virtual Summit**: Host a virtual summit that consists of multiple webinars or sessions on a particular theme or topic. Participants can purchase an all-access pass to attend the summit, gaining access to all the sessions and exclusive bonus content.

33. **Premium Recording Packages:** Offer premium recording packages that include access to recordings of past webinars, along with additional resources, transcripts, or bonus materials. This appeals to individuals who may have missed the live webinar or want to revisit the content.

34. **Expert Panel or Roundtable Discussions**: Organize expert panel or roundtable discussions as webinars and charge participants to attend these exclusive sessions. Curate a panel of industry experts who can share insights and engage in valuable discussions.

35. **Consulting Packages**: Offer consulting packages or personalized sessions as an upsell or add-on to your webinars. Participants can purchase one-on-one consulting time with you to receive personalized advice or guidance related to the webinar topic.

36. **Certification or Continuing Education Credits**: Develop webinars that provide continuing education credits or certifications in partnership with industry

associations or organizations. Professionals seeking to maintain their certifications or fulfill education requirements can attend and pay for these accredited webinars.

37. **Sponsored Webinar Series:** Partner with sponsors or brands to create a sponsored webinar series. Each webinar in the series can focus on a specific topic or theme related to the sponsor's industry or offerings. The sponsor provides financial support in exchange for branding and promotional opportunities.

38. **High-Level Masterclasses**: Create high-level masterclass webinars that delve deeply into advanced topics or niche areas. Position these webinars as premium offerings, charging a higher price due to the specialized and advanced nature of the content.

39. **Paywall or Membership Site:** Establish a paywall or membership site where participants must subscribe or pay a recurring fee to access your library of recorded webinars or ongoing live sessions. This provides a consistent revenue stream and encourages participants to become long-term subscribers.

40. **Sponsored Polls or Surveys**: Incorporate sponsored polls or surveys within your webinar and offer companies the opportunity to sponsor these interactive

elements. Participants can respond to the polls or surveys while the sponsor receives valuable data or insights.

41. **Targeted Advertising**: Explore the possibility of displaying targeted advertisements during your webinars. Advertisers can pay to have their ads shown to your webinar audience, providing an additional revenue stream.

42. **Through podcast**: Making money with webinars through a podcast involves integrating webinars into your podcast content and using various strategies to monetize them. Here's how you can do it:
Plan Webinar Episodes: Design episodes that revolve around webinar-style content, such as expert interviews, panel discussions, or deep dives into specific topics. Ensure the podcast episodes are informative, engaging, and align with your target audience's interests.

Promote Webinars within Podcasts: Mention upcoming webinars or webinar replays during your podcast episodes. Encourage listeners to register for your webinars to gain more in-depth insights on the discussed topics.

Offer Premium Webinars: Consider offering premium or exclusive webinars to your podcast audience. These webinars could feature extended content, Q&A sessions, or access to special guests, and require a fee for registration.

Utilize Podcast Show Notes: Include links to webinar registrations, landing pages, or resources related to the podcast content in your show notes. This makes it easy for listeners to access your webinars.

Cross-Promote with Webinar Hosts: Collaborate with webinar hosts or organizations to feature their webinars as exclusive podcast content. In return, they can promote your podcast to their audience, expanding your listener base.

Sponsorship Opportunities: Attract sponsors or advertisers who are interested in reaching your podcast audience. Offer sponsorship packages that include promotion of their webinars or events during your podcast episodes.

Create Webinar Series: Host a series of webinars that complements your podcast content. For example, if your podcast focuses on personal finance, create a webinar series on budgeting, investing, and saving strategies.

Build a Podcast Community: Foster a dedicated podcast community by engaging with your listeners through social media and email newsletters. Offer special perks, like early access to webinar registrations, to loyal listeners.

Monetize Through Membership Programs: Offer premium podcast content or additional benefits through a membership program. Include access to exclusive webinars as part of the membership package.

Leverage Podcast Analytics: Use podcast analytics to track listener engagement and identify popular topics. Tailor your webinars based on this data to cater to your audience's preferences and interests.

Create Webinar Promotional Episodes: Create podcast episodes solely dedicated to promoting your upcoming webinars. Share insights, testimonials, and highlights from past webinars to entice listeners to attend.

Repurpose Webinar Content into Podcasts: Repurpose valuable content from your webinars into podcast episodes. This allows you to reach a broader audience and provide a taste of the webinar experience to potential attendees.

By integrating webinars into your podcast strategy and leveraging your podcast's audience reach, you can monetize your content while providing valuable insights and experiences to your listeners. Focus on delivering high-quality webinars that align with your podcast theme and cater to your audience's needs. With consistent effort and strategic promotion, webinars can become a lucrative revenue stream for your podcasting endeavors.

Example
Let's consider an example of how a podcast host in the personal development niche can make money with webinars through their podcast:

Example: Personal Development Podcast with Webinar Monetization

Podcast Theme: The podcast host focuses on personal development topics, covering subjects like mindset, goal setting, time management, and building self-confidence.

Engaging Webinar Episodes: The host plans podcast episodes that are in-depth discussions with experts in the personal development field. Each episode provides valuable insights and actionable advice to help listeners improve various aspects of their lives.

Webinar Promotion: During the podcast episodes, the host mentions upcoming webinars on specific personal development topics. They encourage listeners to register for these webinars to dive deeper into the subjects discussed in the episodes.

Premium Webinars: The host offers premium webinars that provide more in-depth content, interactive exercises, and personalized Q&A sessions with the experts. These premium webinars require a fee for registration.

Sponsors and Advertisers: The podcast attracts sponsors and advertisers interested in reaching the personal development audience. Some sponsors may be personal development coaches, authors, or organizations that host webinars themselves.

Sponsored Webinar Content: The host collaborates with sponsoring organizations to feature their webinars as exclusive podcast content. This includes webinars hosted by the sponsors on personal development-related topics.

Membership Program: The podcast offers a membership program for dedicated listeners. Members gain access to exclusive episodes, early webinar registrations, and discounts on premium webinars.

Webinar Series: The host organizes a series of webinars that align with the podcast's key themes. For example, they might have a webinar series on "Mastering Mindfulness" or "Productivity Hacks for Success."

Podcast Community: The host builds a dedicated podcast community through social media, email newsletters, and a private forum. They engage with listeners, share webinar updates, and offer special perks for community members.

Repurposed Content: Valuable insights and takeaways from webinars are repurposed into podcast episodes. This provides a teaser for the full webinar experience and encourages listeners to attend future webinars.

Webinar Promotion Episodes: The host creates podcast episodes solely dedicated to promoting upcoming webinars. They share success stories and testimonials from past webinar attendees to showcase the value of the events.

Webinar Analytics: The host utilizes webinar analytics to track attendee engagement, feedback, and overall success. This data helps them refine their webinar content and improve future webinars.

Through a strategic integration of webinars into their podcast, the personal development podcast host generates revenue from premium webinars, sponsorships, and membership programs. They provide valuable content to their audience while building a thriving podcast community and a profitable webinar-based revenue stream.

Remember to consider your target audience, their preferences, and the value you provide when choosing the most suitable monetization strategies for your webinars. Experiment with different approaches, track the results, and adjust your strategies as needed to optimize your webinar monetization efforts.

Conclusion:

Congratulations! You have reached the end of "How to Make Money with Webinars: Unlocking Profitable Opportunities." Throughout this course, we have explored the strategies, techniques, and best practices that can help you transform your webinars into lucrative revenue streams.

We began by understanding the importance of choosing the right webinar platform, considering your target audience, and creating high-quality content that engages and resonates with your viewers. We explored effective promotional strategies to drive attendance and maximize the reach of your webinars. By putting your passion, expertise, and market demands into consideration, you can position yourself as a valuable resource and attract a loyal audience.

We also delved into the significance of delivering quality webinar content, incorporating eye-catching visuals, and continuously refining your approach based on participant feedback. By staying attuned to the needs and preferences of your audience, you can create compelling learning experiences that keep them coming back for more.

Furthermore, we examined various monetization strategies, such as selling your webinars, offering membership programs, leveraging affiliate marketing, and collaborating with sponsors or brands. Each method presents unique opportunities to generate revenue and unlock the full potential of your webinars.

Remember, success in monetizing webinars requires continuous learning, experimentation, and adaptation. Stay informed about industry trends, embrace new technologies and tools, and always strive to deliver value to your audience.

Now armed with the knowledge and skills gained from this course, you are well-prepared to embark on your journey to make money with webinars. Put your newfound insights into action, remain persistent, and don't be afraid to think outside the box.

Thank you for joining us on this exciting learning adventure. We wish you every success in harnessing the power of webinars to achieve your financial goals. Get ready to make an impact, inspire your audience, and watch your webinar endeavors flourish. Best of luck on your webinar monetization journey!